F

POETRY TREE

Helen V. Burton

VANTAGE PRESS
New York

FIRST EDITION

Copyright © 1997 by Helen V. Burton

Published by Vantage Press, Inc.
516 West 34th Street, New York, New York 10001

Manufactured in the United States of America
ISBN: 0-533-11795-X

Library of Congress Catalog Card No.: 95-90968

0 9 8 7 6 5 4 3 2 1

Contents

Introduction

You're invited to climb
My Poetry Tree
It was planted specially
For you—by me

It's filled with poems about many things
From collecting to traveling
To seasons and siblings

It's about my experiences
Thoughts and feelings
Straight from the heart
And quite revealing

If you read them carefully
You'll learn about me
Look for me there
In the Poetry Tree

So climb it with pleasure
And as you ascend
May you sense joy and peace
That will never end

POETRY TREE

Joy of Living

The joy of giving
is the joy of living.

The act of taking
Is like forsaking—

The principle of sharing
The principle of caring.

When we extend ourselves
and reach out
We receive much more
without a doubt.

The joy of giving
Is the joy of living.

That's Love, That's Life

Joy, pain, sun, rain
That's Life.

Hearts laughing
Hearts crying
Hearts living
Hearts dying
That's Love.

Ups, downs, smiles, frowns
That's Life.

Some working
Some playing
Some measuring
Some weighing
That's Life.

Whether it's Life
Whether it's Love
We know that both
Come from above.

Take a Walk

When you feel tired
and want to be inspired
TAKE A WALK

When your spirits are low
And you've nowhere to go
TAKE A WALK

When you are confused
You may be amused
If you TAKE A WALK

When you want to be stimulated
And feel invigorated
TAKE A WALK

If you are so sad
And want to be glad
TAKE A WALK

You may meet a date
Or even a mate
When you TAKE A WALK

You'll have no regrets
Though you may sweat
When you TAKE A WALK

Alone

Sometimes it's nice to be alone
with no one else but you.
With your own thoughts, no interruptions
Your outlook you'll renew.

It's fun to talk to oneself sometimes
A one-way conversation,
Sometimes it's humorous, sometimes serious
But no mis-communication.

No one to ask you questions
No one to yell or scream;
It is so refreshing sometimes
To be a one-person team.

Do and say just what you want,
Function at your own speed;
Cry or laugh, smile or frown,
Depending on your need.

You only need to please yourself
When you are alone.
And, please remember whatever you do
DO NOT ANSWER THE PHONE.

On Collecting

People collect a variety of things,
Bells, animals, boats, etchings.

They collect whatever brings them pleasure,
Things for many years to treasure.

Stamps and coins are common items
That people collect ad infinitum.

Antiques are collected by those who say
They will increase—in value some day.

My special collection consists of vases;
I've brought home from 100 places.

Are you one who likes to collect?
Unusual things that you elect?

I asked my friend what she collects;
She gave me a reply I did not expect.

She said, "Collectibles only gather dust
So I only collect things that I must."

She gave me no further explanation
So again, I asked her for clarification.

She said, "I only collect things I can use
Such as the latest fashions, especially shoes."

So to each their own in what they invest;
I like my collection of vases best.

To a Friend

I owe you a debt of gratitude,
To me you're always kind.
If I searched all day and night
No better friend could I find.

You listen to me when I am down
And never turn away;
I've come to depend so much on you
To support me along the way.

You're so compassionate, always giving,
Forever understanding;
Unselfish in your attitude;
Never are you demanding.

You seem to know my every mood
And when I am upset
You offer consolation;
You've never failed me yet.

Sometimes I wonder how you can be
So calm and so serene
When I must gather all my strength
Just to avoid a scene.

Things must sometimes bother you
Though it never shows.
How you manage always to smile
God only knows.

You are a great role model
For everyone you touch;
You set such a good example
and I thank you VERY MUCH.

Siblings

Though I may be youngest of 13
I was always heard and always seen.

Growing up the youngest was a party for me;
There were no problems—none I could see.

It seems I was granted my every request;
My brothers and sisters all liked me best.

My brothers frequently took me on their dates;
I felt so lucky—Boy! Did I rate!

Their girlfriends didn't mind—they cared about me too;
They related to me—like big sisters do.

My four big sisters were often like mothers,
Loving, caring, just like my brothers.

They shared so much and there's no doubt
In giving to me—themselves went without.

What they all sacrificed—I was not aware;
They made life for me—more than fair.

I am so lucky to be the youngest of 13,
I am still always heard and always seen.

What If?

What if skies weren't blue
And one meant two.

What if birds didn't sing
And bells didn't ring.

What if summer were cold
And young meant old.

What if clouds were brown
And up meant down.

What if giants were small
And spring meant fall.

What if work meant play
And night meant day.

What if fat meant thin
And out meant in.

What if left meant right
And black meant white.

If all these "ifs" came true
You'd be me and I'd be you.

A topsy-turvy world at best
North would be South and East—West.

So let's not question if hers means his
Let's be content with what is.

My Father

My father, John, I loved him so
Even if he died, long ago.

It happened when I was only seven;
I talk to him often—I know he's in heaven.

Memories of him are vivid and strong;
He always taught me right from wrong.

I think I was the favorite child;
His temperament to me was mild.

From work he'd come—up the hill;
I would run and meet him—what a thrill!

He'd swoop me up—with a hug and kiss—
Such an impact—I've not forgotten this.

He was handsome, gentle, really quite tall;
When I climbed his legs—I had a ball!

He worked hard every day—though I was unaware
Of sacrifices he made to give us good care.

He shared what he had with anyone in need;
I saw many times the people he'd feed.

His untimely departure left me so much pain
But wonderful memories will always remain.

On Being Alone

Sometimes I like to be alone,
No television, no telephone

No noises of any kind,
I just sit and clear my mind

The sound of quiet gives me peace
All my stress to release

This time alone is so special to me;
Some may wonder, "How can it be?"

It is good to be alone,
No radio, no telephone

They might ask, "What would you do—
When there is no one but you?"

Just why it's great—I can't explain;
It's simply pure pleasure—never pain

If you try, then you'll know
Why sometimes, ALONE is the way to go.

Football Widow

During football season I'm often alone
Even though my husband's home.

For hours at football games he stares;
I might as well not even be there.

Darn that television set!
Stiffest competition I've ever met.

Not just one but many games;
To me they all look just the same.

A bunch of men running around,
Pushing and screaming and falling down.

Sometimes kicking an odd-shaped ball;
A series of numbers someone calls.

The concentration drives me insane;
From anger sometimes I can't refrain.

I think it's proper that I mention
I feel alone—and want attention.

Sometimes I leave and hope he'll see
That football comes between him and me.

It has not worked, 'cause upon my return
He hasn't missed me, I'm sad to learn.

I don't think I really hate football
But I really prefer shopping at the mall.

Watching just one game would be just fine
And the rest of the day—his and mine.

But he's not convinced of this just yet;
If you can help me, I'll be in your debt.

Am I alone? Are there others like me
Who feel alone and somewhat empty?

I have an idea—we'll play our own game
Our own little group—we'll have our own name;
Anyone can join who finds football a bore
Never to be—alone anymore.

Birthdays

Birthdays can be a lot of fun;
Do you admit you still have one?

The gifts, cards, the congratulations
Are all part of this celebration.

No matter the month, no matter the day,
Mondays in March or Fridays in May.

Enjoy it fully—spare no expense;
Do as you please—you need no defense.

Eat what you like—have a drink or two;
You can't go wrong, in whatever you do.

You'll get plenty of special attention;
Birthdays are such a great invention!

A time to let it all hang out;
Fun time is what it's all about.

For me, it's the best day of the year
With memories that I'll hold so dear.

So, cherish each birthday, celebrate! Have a blast!
For you don't know, which one will be the last.

Baking

When I can't sleep, I simply bake;
Then I no longer lie awake.

My family awakens to the smells;
They say they're checking to see if I'm well.

I have to convince them I am fine
And baking gives me peace of mind.

Pound cakes, I find easy to do
But cookies give satisfaction too.

I bake until I run out of steam
Then I have such pleasant dreams.

Baking for me is not a chore
And never, never is a bore.

From baking, I derive so much joy,
Just like a child with a brand new toy.

The aroma makes some salivate
And anxious to indulge—can hardly wait.

So many choices, so many treats,
So many delicious things to eat.

Though resisting temptation should be my goal
I have very little self-control.

So I'll need to keep in mind
It is in baking, where peace I find,

And give the goodies to my friends
And let THEM worry about double chins.

Dr. Ann

I have a wonderful daughter,
Her name is Dr. Ann;
Although she doesn't know it
I'm her biggest fan.

She has talent, brains and good looks,
She's hard-working and dedicated;
Her common sense is overwhelming
And she's so appreciated.

Though she is an Only child
She's never ever been spoiled;
She is quite independent,
From challenges has never recoiled.

She's adventuresome and curious,
Loves caring for the sick;
Sometimes she's so complicated
I wonder what makes her tick.

She usually sings in private,
A beautiful contralto voice;
Every time I hear it
I simply must rejoice!

She was anxious to arrive
And was born two weeks early;
From the moment she debuted
I've loved her very dearly.

She said, "Hi, World, it's Ann."
What a glorious greeting;
She's brought me so much joy
I think she's worth repeating.

Her favorite toys were Lego
Tammy dolls, puzzles too;
She often entertained herself
Found interesting things to do.

Though she played with other children
She often played alone,
For when she tired of others
She told them to "go home."

She was not a "terrible two"
Nor a "frustrating three."
She was a "trusting four,"
And happy as could be.

From about the age of five
Up to the age of nine
She seemed to be contented
And everything was fine.

And then I went out to work
A career to pursue;
She expressed such disapproval
I didn't know what to do.

At work I felt so guilty,
Thought of her all day long;
I wondered if she was okay,
Was my decision wrong?

I sought advice from friends
And colleagues I could trust;
They said, "Please don't feel guilty;
Ann will soon adjust."

So carefully I explained to her
Why my choice was right;
Such a traumatic time,
I failed to sleep some nights.

Finally I gained her support
And we went on our way
To bigger and better things
We still enjoy today.

She warned me as she entered her teens
What there was in store;
Not only did she follow through
But oh, so much, much, more!

She certainly was not a typical teen,
Was wise beyond her years;
I worried about her growing up so soon,
I had so many fears.

But she got through those years okay,
From her I learned so much
And far, far too often
I made mistakes, blunders and such.

I sometimes feel she matured so fast
Was not long enough a "Kid."
Was this a natural phenomenon
Or was it something I did?

Today she seems well on her way
To achieving her special goal
And I wish her only the very best
With all my heart and soul.

And now there's nothing more to say
Except express my pride,
ANN, you're Super Special
And I'll be always by your side.

You've worked, struggled and sacrificed
You've made it—and HOW!
So my Precious Dr. Ann,
Please take a bow.

The Sad One

There's a sadness in his eyes,
Seems it's been there for a while
And sometimes it also appears
There's a pain behind his smile.

Though he's friendly and polite
To those he is around
I believe sometimes that
He'd secretly prefer to frown.

It seems he may have suffered hurt
Somewhere along the way;
Something happened in the past
That makes him sad today.

He often seems so far away
And really not in touch;
To know his thoughts and feelings
I'd like very much.

If he would only tell me
What's really bothering him,
What he's thinking, what's on his mind,
Could it be that grim!

If he could only open up,
If only he would share,
He'd find a true and concerned friend
And that someone really cares.

I wonder how long he's been this way
And if there's any cure
How long he can continue,
How much he can endure?

I want so much to offer help
But simply don't know how;
Would he accept my interference?
Is this something he'd allow?

But for now, I'll offer a smile
And make my presence known
And hopefully he'll soon realize
That he is not alone.

Walking

Go for a walk and you will find
It frees the spirit, clears the mind.

You need not have a destination;
You'll rid yourself of much frustration.

It takes the clutter from your path,
Leaves it clean, like taking a bath.

Removes anger, brings calm,
It soothes; it's a natural balm.

Separates trivia from sublime,
It's such a healthy use of time.

You need no special walking gear,
Just be comfortable in what you wear.

Walk with groups, crowds or pairs
Or if you prefer—Solitaire.

Walking gives me such a high
I feel I'm reaching for the sky.

I find it gives me such great pleasure,
Its value one just cannot measure.

Advantages of walking are so many,
It doesn't even cost a penny!

Such a feeling of exhilaration
And it generates inspiration.

Walk for fun, not competition,
Get rid of all those inhibitions.

Begin your walk when you are sad,
When you finish, you'll be glad.

Walking cannot be praised enough,
It smooths things when times are tough.

Walking is so good for all,
The young, old, short and tall.

So walk as much as time allows,
Go ahead—begin right now!

I hope you're convinced and will agree
To go out walking someday with me.

Moderation

It's so easy to overindulge;
When food's the culprit, you'll get a bulge.

If alcohol you're inclined to drink
It impairs your normal ability to think.

Staying up too late means too little sleep,
Makes the next day's appointments difficult to keep.

Sitting too long is less than wise;
Why not get some exercise?

Overworking may mean your heart you'll tax;
Why not learn just to relax?

On the other hand, too much play
May interfere with a productive day.

Study too hard and you will find
May tend to overstretch the mind.

But if you fail to study at all
It could result in your downfall.

Be neither too fast not too slow;
Aim neither too high nor too low.

So practice moderation in all you do;
You'll see that this is best for you.

Seasons

Most folks think
There are only four.
I'd like to add
Just one more.

I call it something
In between.
It can only be felt
But never seen.

It's neither hot nor cold
Nor warm, nor cool.
It's something you don't
Learn in school.

It's mysterious, exciting,
Joyful and new.
It makes one change
One's point of view.

For this fifth season
Has no name
It's still important
Just the same.

It's real
And not my imagination.
It's wonderful, grand
A big SENSATION!

I still love summer, spring
Winter and fall.
But I love the fifth season
Best of all.

Miss Piggy

Miss Piggy is such a Unique Cat,
She eats too much, thus is too fat.

No matter what I feed her, it's never enough,
She eats many things, all kinds of stuff.

Yet she's picky in many ways,
Eats certain foods on certain days.

She fills her tummy then goes to sleep,
For she has no promises to keep.

She's at my door every morn,
Whining and screaming, like a newborn,

Demanding I pay attention to her;
When I respond, she begins to purr.

Displays her tummy for a rubdown;
She must be the laziest cat in town.

Her tigerlike expression is scary sometimes,
Makes one wonder what's on her mind.

She's sometimes sneaky, challenges my trust,
Yet punishing her seems unjust.

She likes to hide among clean clothes;
It's one of her favorite places to doze.

She goes outside but stays near home;
She seems to have no desire to roam.

She loves to lie on my neighbor's step
And hold her prisoner till she asks for help.

You see, my neighbor is afraid of cats
So naturally Miss Piggy is aware of that.

She takes advantage of my neighbor's fear;
I'm sure if we'd move, my neighbor would cheer.

When Piggy must go to the vet for care
She seems to question, "*Must* I go there?"

She resists these visits with all her might;
My attempts at this result in fights.

She hates car rides, makes quite a fuss
So we only take her when we must.

She'd rather stay home and lie around
And keep on gaining—pound after pound.

She is sure to pout, when I get home late;
She just stands at the door and waits.

When I don't arrive at *her* expected time
She just ignores me, treats me like SLIME.

After a while she warms up to me;
She snuggles and is friendly as can be.

I could go on about Piggy the Cat,
How she uses people like they're door mats.

That softness to the touch, that pitiful purr,
How could anyone dislike her?

So My Dear Piggy—I'll just stay cool
And continue to follow "Miss Piggy's Rules."

Education

If you want to grow
In wisdom and in knowledge
First, complete high school
Then go on to college.

If you want an education
You must study at every chance;
If you work very hard
Your knowledge you'll enhance.

Learning is ongoing,
A never-ending process;
If you want to advance
And never to regress.

Learning is hard for some,
For others it comes with ease;
You must make every effort
If yourself you want to please.

Traveling

I love to travel. It's such great fun.
Of my favorite hobbies, it's number ONE!

Staying home can be a bore;
Traveling makes me grow much more.

I see places and things that are new to me,
Things that I thought that I would never see.

People of all colors, religions and backgrounds,
Speaking many languages—spending rupees, pesos and
pounds.

Dressed in varied clothing—fascinating to see,
Eating many foods of great variety.

Friendly and curious, sometimes simple stares
Give an indication—we are all from everywhere!

Travel by any mode, water, land, or air—
As long as I can travel—I really do not care.

Explore the different cultures, is what I like most;
I've had some neat experiences, though I do not like to
boast.

I've taken many pictures and collected souvenirs;
They've kept memories alive—all through the years.

And though I like to travel and far away to roam
I must confess to you, it's nice when I get home.

Travel to Europe, Asia, Africa—anywhere you may
But there is just no other place like the good OLD USA.

My Friend Jesse

I'll tell you about my friend Jesse,
He's not easy to get to know;
He rarely smiles at anyone
And his pace is now quite slow.

Though he may be kind and gentle
And never shows aggression,
When you look at him you'll see
His face shows no expression.

He enjoys a good discussion,
He's an expert in everything;
He also likes to argue
And thinks he is a King.

His devoted wife is Clyde,
She just can't figure him out;
Can anyone help us find
What Jesse is all about?

You'll find him tall and handsome
If Jesse you should meet;
He usually likes to stay at home
In his special seat.

Fresh fruit and roast turkey
Are some foods he likes;
His favorite TV channel is "4."
He may watch it day or night.

He only talks when he gets ready
But when he does, Watch Out!
If something's said he doesn't like
It just might make him pout.

Say what you want about my friend Jesse,
He's still just fine by me;
When everyone else sees him frown
It's really a smile I see.

Camp Seagull

A safe and relaxing atmosphere,
Nothing to cause one to fear.

Many activities from which to choose
From sleeping in, to a sailing cruise.

Aerobics, crafts, water sports
Numerous activities of all sorts.

Sandy beach and lots, lots more,
Being at camp is never a bore.

Morning walks begin the day,
Exercise classes or sports to play.

Meals are planned with health in mind,
Rich desserts you'll never find.

Show-time gives us all a chance
To be creative as we dance.

Cabin skits are such fun;
We try to involve everyone.

Charlevoix walks challenge the bold
Whether we're young or whether we're old.

Meeting new campers is always a treat;
Their enthusiasm just can't be beat.

Camping staff are top of the line;
They make you feel special all the time.

They pamper us royally from the time we arrive;
We want to stay there till we're ninety-five?

I look forward to going to Seagull each year,
Nothing to cause one to fear.

Excess Baggage

When one's baggage is in excess
And is heavy on the heart
It makes one's burdens seem endless
And slows attempts to start.

It tires the mind, the heart, and soul
And injures body too;
It changes happiness to sadness
And makes successes few.

One cannot carry excess baggage
And expect to get ahead,
For excess baggage can weigh one down
Like 100 lbs. of lead.

Normal baggage is just fine;
X-tra baggage?—NO!!
So raise your spirit upward
Never let it get low.

Accept only what's important to you,
Reject the negative game;
Be kind to you, accept reality,
No reason to feel ashamed.

So throw away that excess baggage;
Carry only what you need
To get you in, over and through
Do yourself a good deed.

You'll do quite well with lighter weight
As you live fully each day.
And realize then that excess baggage
Was only in your way.

Why?

Why do birds sing
And fly across the sky?
Why do bells ring
From towers up so high?

Why do soldiers fight?
Make war instead of peace.
Why do some dogs bite
Their anger to release?

Why do babies crawl
And cause us so much worry?
Why are grown-ups irritable
When they are in a hurry?

Why do people frown
When they can wear a smile?
Why be always down
When laughter is in style?

Why is winter cold?
Why is summer hot?
Why do some die old?
And other folks do not?

Why do trees grow tall?
Why do rivers run?
Why do leaves?
And there's not always sun?

Why, why, so many whys!
So much I want to know.
I guess I cannot be as wise
As the ONE who runs the show.

God, You and Me
(*The Big Three*)

God, you and me;
We are the BIG THREE.

Not Chrysler, Ford and GM,
No, it's none of them.
It's God, you and me;
We are the BIG THREE.

Cars can only run
And sometimes that's no fun.
'Cause when they're in a hurry
They provoke unnecessary worry.

But God causes no pain
And with us shall remain.
God walks with you and me;
We follow faithfully.

For when we follow God
We're led all the way
And watched over constantly
In all we do and say.

If there were no God
There'd be no you and me;
Then of course you know
There would be no "BIG 3."

He

When he walked into my life one day
And looked at me in a special way,

He exuded charm, warmth and joy
Somewhat like that of a little boy.

I felt something different; did I dare let on—
If I hesitated too long would he be gone?

I caught sight of his boyish smile;
I decided I'd chance to visit awhile.

I think he knew, just as did I
That this was special—I breathed a sigh.

He held my hand; I held his too.
We felt each other's love deeply and knew.

We'd found that Special, Special thing—
That only truth and love can bring.

Our dreams, hopes and thoughts we shared;
He listened intently—I knew he cared.

And now, we're committed to each other forever
Never to part—NEVER, NEVER, NEVER!!

Shapes

I would not like to be a circle
'Cause I'd go 'round and 'round
Like a dog chasing his tail
Until it wears him down.

A square has four sides
All of them the same;
Many things are shaped like this
Including a picture frame.

Triangles have three points
But what use can they be?
It's just as well to have
Two points, rather than three.

Then there is the rectangle;
Like a square, its sides are four;
It's a useful shape
And reminds me of a door.

A pentagon has five sides;
Interesting—some say
But it makes little sense to me
Why it's shaped this way.

Hexagons, octagons,
Many other shapes you see
Are just too complicated
To be described by me.

I'm sure that every shape created
Circles, triangles or square
All have meaning to someone
'Cause they're found everywhere.

Money and Friendship

There was a man of wealth;
He was a multimillionaire.
He thought he had no worries
And hadn't many cares.

But he found his friends were phonies;
All were insincere,
For when he needed them the most
They were never there.

He found they showed no support
In the time of need.
They were all so selfish
And overcome with greed.

He found they only wished
To be on the receiving end.
To take and never give
Seemed to be the trend.

He learned a bitter lesson
But it did not turn him sour;
It only made him wiser
And gave him more power.

He made all new friends
Who knew not of his riches.
For all they knew, he earned his living
By simply digging ditches.

He found these friends to be true
Unique with qualities so rare,
For they were rich in love and spirit,
Showed support, concern and care.

If you'll remember this
Friendship you will win.
True riches come not from money
But rather from within.

I Hate Being Ill

Confined to bed
Nose runny
Eyes red
I hate being ill.

Shivering and cold
Must lie down
Feeling so old
Why am I ill?

Coughing and sneezing
Head aching
Gasping and wheezing
I don't want to be ill.

No appetite
Feeling miserable
No sleep at night
Being ill is the pits!

Body so sore
Can hardly move
It's such a bore
Do I have to be ill?

In so much pain
I want to be well
Once again
Have you ever been ill?

Thought I'd be well
In a day or two
Being ill is hell
I detest being ill.

What a mess
I've got to improve
So much stress
I d-o-n'-t l-i-k-e b-e-i-n-g i-l-l.

Lying in bed and feeling crummy
Pins and needles in my throat
Butterflies in my tummy
Why must I be ill?

I know it's temporary
But still it's inconvenient
Out of the ordinary
I hate being ill.

I'll change my attitude—look on the bright side;
I'm still living and in life hope resides
So there's no need to hate being ill.

Cat Slave

Being a slave to a cat
Means responding to its beck and call
Trying to meet its every need
And giving it your all.

I'm sure you know just what I mean
When I tell you about my cat
How she controls my life
If you can imagine that.

She sends me to the store quite often
To purchase her special food;
If I fail to get the kind she likes
She develops a foul mood.

She loves to watch from under the table
While lying in a chair;
As long as she sees me moving about
She doesn't seem to care.

But just as soon as I try to relax
She begins her little play
Demanding attention, some affection
She clearly does enjoy.

When I'm not looking, she's on the furniture
Claiming it as her own;
She also takes advantage of me
When I'm on the telephone.

Her milk must be the right temperature
In order for her to drink it;
Can you imagine this from a cat—
Who would ever think it?

She only likes things that are clean;
This includes fresh laundry too
So I keep my linen closet closed
Or the laundry I have to redo!

She lies in doorways and hallways
Making her difficult to ignore;
I must stop to pet and talk to her,
She's just "ROTTEN" to the core.

I sometimes lie on the floor
To read or watch TV
But the cat only wants the spot I'm in;
Has no regard for me.

Yes, I'm a slave to my cat
And will probably never be free
'Cause that's the way cats are made—
And I'm only human you see.

To Sven

I boarded the *Academic Ioffe*
An Antarctica cruise to take;
I had no idea what was in store
Or what new friends I'd make.

They came from many nations
With enthusiasm on their faces
Of various ethnic backgrounds
And of different religions and races.

They were such interesting people
Well traveled except for a few;
Most I found quite friendly
Warm and likeable too.

But one in the crowd stood out,
I learned his name was Sven;
Such a kindly face
The gentlest of men.

He made everyone feel comfortable
Showed concern for us all;
It was always quite obvious
That he was having a ball.

He challenged all the lecturers
With one more question to ask;
They welcomed his inquisitive nature
And gladly took him to task.

Sven always enjoyed singing
And reciting poems to me
While his lovely and understanding wife
Smiled at him patiently.

Sven rarely ever complained
Took everything in stride;
I think he is a person
In whom one could confide.

He told me about his cat
Its name and the reason why;
Some would find it humorous
But it made me want to cry.

Sven is such a sensitive person
Related well to everyone;
He always wanted to make sure
That we were having fun.

He made my experience very special;
I want to go to Antarctica again
But I hope when I read the passenger list
The first name listed is Sven.

Affectionately,

Helen